Series / Number 90-014

Citizens, Leaders, and Legislators: *Perspectives on Support for the American Legislature*

SAMUEL C. PATTERSON

G. R. BOYNTON

University of Iowa

SAGE PUBLICATIONS / Beverly Hills / London

For information address:

SAGE PUBLICATIONS, INC.
275 South Beverly Drive
Beverly Hills, California 90212

SAGE PUBLICATIONS LTD.
St George's House / 44 Hatton Garden
London EC1N 8ER

International Standard Book Number 0-8039-0484-3

Library of Congress Catalog No. L.C. 74-19989

FIRST PRINTING

When citing a professional paper, please use the proper form. Remember to cite the
correct Sage Professional Paper series title and include the paper number. One of the
two following formats can be adapted (depending on the style manual used):

(1) KORNBERG, A. et al. (1973) "Legislatures and Societal Change: The Case of
Canada." Sage Research Papers in the Social Sciences (Comparative Legislative
Studies Series, No. 90-002). Beverly Hills and London: Sage Pubns.

OR

(2) Kornberg, Allan et al. 1973. *Legislatures and Societal Change: The Case of
Canada.* Sage Research Papers in the Social Sciences, vol. 1, series no. 90-002
(Comparative Legislative Studies Series). Beverly Hills and London: Sage Publications.

Contents

99322

SAMUEL C. PATTERSON is Professor of Political Science and Chairman of the Department at the University of Iowa. He is the co-author of The Legislative Process in the United States, *and editor of* American Legislative Behavior *and of* Comparative Legislative Behavior. *His research interests and publications have included various aspects of interest groups at the national and state level, state politics, and studies of legislative support in Iowa and in a sample of American states.*

G. R. BOYNTON is Professor of Political Science and Director of the Laboratory for Political Research at the University of Iowa. His research interests have been focused on public opinion, comparative legislative behavior, and legislative support, and he has published widely on these topics in various political science journals.

CITIZENS, LEADERS, AND LEGISLATORS:
Perspectives on Support for
the American Legislature

SAMUEL C. PATTERSON and
G. R. BOYNTON

University of Iowa

I. INTRODUCTION

Political systems or subsystems, like institutions of all kinds, require public support in order to survive, to achieve their goals, or to perform effectively. Schools, churches, community chests, and social clubs all require and ordinarily seek support among their own members, among potential members, and in the community at large. Withdrawal of support on a large scale from such organized groups or institutions usually means their demise. In a somewhat similar way, legislatures require support in order to persist, to deal with public- and organized-group demands effectively, to make necessary political decisions. In this respect, legislatures probably do not differ from a wide variety of organized groups and institutions (Blom, 1970: 110-111). But, of course, legislatures more than most public and private groups, and more than the bureaucratic or judicial branches of the government, are representative political institutions. In the American setting they are supposed to represent the people as they are divided into equal-population districts, and by and large they do so. The crucial representative role of legislatures is such that support for the entire political system may well hinge upon support for the most representative agency. The legislature confers legitimacy and authority upon governmental acts, so that support for it is particularly vital for the effective performance of the system as a whole (Loewenberg, 1973: 142-43; 1971: 177-200; Muller, 1970: 1149-1152).

In this report, we establish the basis for measuring supportive attitudes toward the legislature, and make comparisons between samples of the general public and political-elite groups in their distributions of legislative support.[1] Then, we show what perspectives our respondents have of the critical attributes and motives of legislative representatives, and what orientations respondents have of both the adequacy of representation and the efficacy of compromise in legislative decision-making. Taking support for the legislature as our dependent variable, we show to what extent independent variables associated with citizens' and leaders' perspectives of the legislators and legislative work account for variations in support. Our inquiry demonstrates, in one context, how much support for the legislative assembly flows from constituents' perspectives about the kinds of people who are and should be legislators, their belief about the motivations legislators have for candidacy for office, and their general notions about the adequacy of legislative representation and the basis of decision-making.

In this analysis we have drawn upon our earlier reports, especially to the extent that it has been necessary here to recapitulate our general conceptualization of diffuse legislative support (see Boynton, Patterson and Hedlund, 1968: 163-173; Patterson, Boynton and Hedlund, 1969: 62-76; Patterson and Boynton, 1969: 243-263; and, Patterson, Wahlke and Boynton, 1973: 282-313). However, in the main our earlier reports focused upon our general population data. Although we draw upon our sample of the general citizenry for illustrative purposes in the analysis which follows, we concentrate upon comparisons between elite samples and the general public. The analytical presentation involves:

(1)   showing the distributions and factors for independent variables for the general population sample, as an example of the shape of the data for the largest sample group;

(2)   indicating similarities and differences between public and elite groups based upon a common factorial analysis of all sample groups; and

(3)   giving the multiple regression results for the sample group.

Finally, we present a multiple regression for the full set of variables considered, showing their combined impact upon diffuse legislative support. But, before presenting these analyses, something needs to be said about the dependent variable in this inquiry—support for the legislature.

II. SUPPORT FOR THE LEGISLATURE

THE NATURE OF SUPPORT

The term representation may be defined in many ways, but essentially it identifies a set of relationships between a political system and its environment. One track these relationships may take is in the form of demands on the political system—demands for recognition, for access, for changes in public policy, for services, for decisions. Another track is that of support. Easton treats support as a major input to the political system. He argues that, in addition to demands, support provides a "summary variable" with which to examine linkages between the political system and its environment. The concept support has been useful to political scientists, in one way or another, in analyses of processes of public policy formulation. Political parties, interest groups, and leaders, among others, seek to build support for certain political alternatives in order to influence the decision-making processes of the legislature. However, support directed toward the legislature as an institution is not limited to a focus upon specific policy alternatives. Easton points out that

> If demands are to be processed into binding decisions, regardless of whose demands they are, it is not enough that support be collected behind them so as to impress the authorities with the need to adopt them as a basis for decisions. Basically, a large proportion of political research has been devoted to just this matter. Studies of voting behavior, interest groups, parties, and legislative analysis have all sought to reveal the way in which support is distributed, shifted, and mobilized behind varying demands (issues) or behind personalities and leadership groups seeking positions of authority. But if the authorities are to be able to make decisions, to get them accepted as binding, and to put them into effect without the extensive use of coercion, solidarity must be developed not only around some set of authorities themselves, but around the major aspects of the system within which the authorities operate (Easton, 1965: 157-158).

One of the major aspects of the political system is the legislative institution, and we are, of course, interested in the ways in which support may become focused around it.

Support in the political environment for a legislative institution may involve favorable feelings and attitudes in regard to the work of the immediate legislative body. In this vein, we might inquire about people's attitudes toward the particular enactments of the last session of the legislature, their feelings about the way in which the legislature performed, or their evaluations of the work of the last legislature as a whole. But, more basically, support for the legislature may involve fundamental attitudes toward the institution as such, apart from a particular manifestation of it. Easton makes this distinction, calling the former *specific* and the latter *diffuse* support. Specific support "flows from the favorable attitudes and predispositions stimulated by outputs that are perceived by members to meet their demands as they arise or in anticipation" (Easton, 1965: 273). Diffuse support is that reservoir of good will which a system may engender, not dependent upon any particular output, and at the extreme mode typified by unquestioning loyalty or patriotism. In this report, we are especially concerned with diffuse support, but we will show that specific and diffuse support can be quite distinct from one another.

We would expect diffuse support to come in two interrelated but distinguishable components. One component, or dimension, of diffuse support should be the extent to which members of a political system are committed to a political institution. At the extreme, the committed person is willing to preserve and maintain an institution no matter what it does, and the uncommitted person is willing for it to be abolished. Another dimension of diffuse support should be that of compliance—willingness to be obedient, to comply with the programs and enactments authorized by the institution. The reservoir of good will which constitutes diffuse support really involves a high degree of commitment to an institution and compliance with its decisions. And, as political leaders seek to mobilize support, it is possible to imagine them doing so in such a way as to stress one or the other of the dimensions of support. Leaders may emphasize institutional commitment. They may engage in behaviors and pursue programs designed to engender positive enthusiasm for the system; they may seek to mobilize the mass population in a commitment to loyalty and involvement in the system. Or, leaders may stress compliance. They may deliberately seek to maintain mass political apathy, to seek to distract mass participation, and to foster unquestioning subservience in circuses and symbols. The point is that, although we would expect them to be related, institutional commitment and compliance can be expected to be discernible dimensions of diffuse legislative support.

In order to gather empirical evidence appropriate to the analysis of support for the legislature, we interviewed citizens and political actors in an American state—Iowa. In November 1966, we interviewed 1,001 adult citizens who constituted a random household probability sample of the population of the state. Then, during the spring of 1967, we interviewed 181 of the 185 members of the Iowa legislature—including 123 House members and 58 senators. We asked them to nominate persons in their own counties who they regarded as politically knowledgeable and aware, and whose advice they might seek about legislative issues or problems. From the more than 600 names given us by legislators, we selected and interviewed 484 nominated constituents who matched the communities in which our general population respondents resided. In the same communities we also interviewed county party chairmen in both major parties if they had not been nominated by legislators as attentive constituents. As such, we have interview materials from a total of 90 out of 198 possible Iowa county party chairmen. Finally, we drew a sample of 100 lobbyists from the lobbyist registration lists prepared by the Chief Clerk of the House of Representatives for the 1967 legislative session, and were able to interview 99 of these lobbyists. The survey schedule for each of these five groups contained a common core of comparable interview items, including several batteries of items involving attitudes toward the legislature. [

MEASUREMENT OF SUPPORT

One indicator of specific legislative support could be simply evaluation of the effectiveness of the legislature in its immediate performance of legislative business. In our 1966 and 1967 interviews, we asked respondents to rate the performance of the legislature, asking whether they thought the last session had done an excellent job, a good job, a fair job, or a poor job. These evaluations provide a rough measure of our respondents' impressions of the adequacy of legislative output, and we take them as useful estimates of specific support for the legislature. The results of asking for such evaluations from the general adult population sample, the party leader sample, the lobbyist sample, and the sample of attentive constituents, are displayed in Table 1. It can be seen that in all groups—for both ordinary citizens in

Table 1 Evaluation of the Legislature in the Mass Public and Among Political Elites

Specific Legislative Support	Mass Public	Party Leaders	Lobbyists	Attentive Constituents
Excellent job	4.8	5.0	2.2	7.3
Good job	49.9	53.2	54.4	61.5
Fair job	41.2	33.4	33.3	25.0
Poor job	4.0	8.4	10.0	6.3
Total	99.9	100.0	100.0	100.1
No. of cases	931	90	96	479

the mass public and those elite groups—evaluations bulge very heavily in the good job and fair job categories. Rather few rate the legislature as excellent. Differences among groups are not extraordinary, although attentive constituents give the legislature a notably higher rating than do other groups. Interestingly, lobbyists are most critical in their evaluations, with 10% of them saying the legislature does a poor job; and fewer lobbyists in percentage terms said the legislature did an excellent job than did other groups.

But, much more than being concerned about comparing public and elite groups in terms of performance evaluation, we are interested in defining, mapping, and attempting to account for variations in diffuse legislative support (Patterson, Wahlke and Boynton, 1973: 291-297). We have attempted to measure underlying support for the legislature as an institution by recording the degree of agreement or disagreement respondents had to seven attitudinal statements, four of which we expected to tap predispositions to comply with the legislative programs and other enactments, and three of which we thought would tap commitment to the legislature itself. These seven statements are spelled out in full in Table 2. That table also shows the most intensively supportive proportions for each group of respondents. The category "most intensively supportive" refers to those who *strongly* agreed or disagreed, depending upon the direction of the item as shown in Table 2.

Although the percentages arrayed in Table 2 make it clear that large proportions of the Iowa samples expressed attitudes of compliance with the laws passed by the legislature, preference for legislative law-making, and commitment to the existence of the legislature as an institution, some notable variations are evident. In the mass public sample, the least legislative support was evinced by the question of the governor taking the law into his own hands rather than waiting for the legislature to act; more than a fourth of the sample agreed that there were times when the governor should do this, and only 12% strongly disagreed. Nearly one-sixth agreed that sometimes citizens should take the law into their own hands without waiting for the legislature to take action, although more than half disagreed and more than a fourth disagreed strongly. In contrast, very marked legislative support was indicated by the high proportions in the public sample who responded in such a way as to show that they felt citizens ought to comply with laws passed by the legislature whether they agreed with them or not. Less than 3% were willing to agree that it was all right to disobey the law. These data suggest that, for some, extraordinary action by the governor or by citizens can sometimes be acceptable substitutes for the legislative process, but outright failure to comply when legislative authority has been exercised rarely is acceptable.

Again, in the public sample the items involving retention of the legislature and reduction of its powers produced greater difficulty in responding—there were more "don't know" responses here—but the pattern for the three items is quite similar for those who did respond. Across these items, about 12% were willing to consider abolishing the legislature or reducing its constitutional powers. More than two-thirds did not wish to reduce legislative power, 72% agreed that proposals to abolish the legislature should be defeated, and more than 78% disagreed with the proposal that the legislature should be abolished if it persistently passed disagreeable laws.

In the elite groups, highly supportive responses were expressed by large proportions of the respondents, compared to the public sample. Thus, from nearly two-thirds up to about three-quarters of the party leaders, attentive constituents, lobbyists, and legislators strongly disagreed with the contention that it was all right to break state laws or for citizens to take the law into their own hands. From nearly a third to about half of

Table 2 Attitudes of Support for the Legislature

Legislative Support Items	Direction of Support	Percent Intensely Supportive				
		Public	Party Leaders	Attentive Con-stituents	Lobby-ists	Legis-lators
If you don't particularly agree with a state law, it is all right to break it if you are careful not to get caught.	Disagree	42.1	58.9	63.2	64.6	71.3
There are times when it almost seems better for the citizens of the state to take the law into their own hands rather than wait for the state legislature to act.	Disagree	28.0	62.2	67.8	73.7	64.6
Even though one might strongly disagree with a state law, after it has been passed by the state legislature one ought to obey it.	Agree	21.6	38.9	41.9	36.4	51.9
If the Iowa legislature continually passed laws that the people disagreed with, it might be better to do away with the legislature altogether.	Disagree	16.4	32.2	37.8	45.5	57.5
There are times when it would almost seem better for the Governor to take the law into his own hands rather than wait for the state legislature to act.	Disagree	11.8	32.2	43.8	52.5	52.5
One should be willing to do everything that he could to make sure that any proposal to abolish the state legislature were defeated.	Agree	9.8	35.6	38.2	32.3	48.6
It would not make much difference if the constitution of Iowa were re-written so as to reduce the powers of the state legislature.	Disagree	6.9	14.4	16.3	20.2	31.5
No. of cases		1,001	90	484	99	181

the respondents in the elite groups took the intensively supportive position for the legislature or authority in question on questions of obeying disagreeable state laws, abolishing the legislature, or the governor taking matters out of legislative hands.

These seven attitudinal items provided a workable basis for indices of diffuse legislative support. For purposes of careful analysis of support, it is desirable to reduce responses to the seven support items to a single score for each respondent. We chose the method of factor analysis to perform this task. Doing so made it feasible to take a close look at the nature of legislative support itself. Our hypotheses about the interrelationships of these seven items were twofold. We first expected that diffuse support for the legislature would form a general dimension. In statistical terms, we expected that the individual attitudinal items would all have high factor loadings on the first factor when subjected to a principal component analysis, and that this factor would account for most of the explained variance. We also thought that this general dimension of support could be divided into two more specific dimensions, which we have already suggested—those of compliance and institutional commitment.

The results of the factor analysis are shown in Table 3, and they are reasonably in accord with our expectations. The table shows each support item, the principal component factor loadings, the loadings for the two-factor rotated solution, and the variance accounted for. By looking at the bottom of Table 3, one can see that our first expectation, that the principal component would produce high loadings for all items, was generally borne out. And, the principal component accounts for more than 70% of the explained variance in every case.

Two factors accounted for around half the total variance in the interrelationships of the seven support items, and ordered these items, in general, in an adequately satisfying way. Looking at the analysis for the mass public, it is plain that the bidimensional character of our support items is confirmed. The first factor is related to the willingness to comply with decisions reached in the legislative system. Four items have high loadings on this factor. Briefly, they are:

(1) There are times when citizens should take the law into their own hands;

(2) It is all right to break the law if you disagree with it;

(3) There are times when the governor should take the law into his own hands; and

(4) One ought to obey laws even if one disagrees.

For the mass public, these four items all had the highest factor loadings on Factor I. Since these four items are directly reflective of compliance with legislative decisions, we call them together the "compliance factor."

Table 3 Dimensions of Legislative Support

Diffuse Legislative Support Items	Mass Public			Party Leaders			Attentive Constituents			Lobbyists			Legislators		
	PC*	I	II	PC	I	II	PC	I	II	PC	I	II	PC	I	II
1 Times when citizens take law into own hands	.591	.745	.033	.678	.800	-.039	.681	.664	.296	.682	.673	-.263	.685	.791	.038
2 All right to break law if you disagree with it	.594	.679	.116	.474	.607	.042	.584	.823	-.002	.631	.169	-.773	.665	.587	.316
3 Times when the Governor should take law into his own hands	.575	.552	.237	.627	.554	-.316	.524	.310	.433	.571	.731	-.025	.696	.798	.047
4 Ought to obey laws even if one disagrees	-.502	-.505	-.180	-.711	-.664	.290	-.621	-.658	-.218	-.576	-.075	.798	-.624	-.531	-.328
5 Ought to do everything to prevent abolishing the legislature	-.482	.015	-.766	-.463	-.019	.782	-.613	-.155	-.716	-.511	-.520	.179	-.611	-.529	-.306
6 If passed laws people disagreed with do away with legislature	.645	.305	.638	.369	.046	-.578	.583	.256	.571	.676	.742	-.174	.650	.309	.719
7 Wouldn't make much difference if legislative powers were reduced	.580	.226	.632	.508	.249	-.530	.525	.001	.745	.554	.253	-.556	.477	.032	.830
% of total variance	70.5			67.9			71.1			71.1			74.3		
% of explained variance		45.9			46.1			49.3			51.2			54.0	

*PC = Principal Component

13

The second factor is related to institutional maintenance. Three items have high loadings on this factor. They are:

(1)   One ought to do everything to prevent abolition of the legislature;

(2)   If it passed laws people disagreed with, better do away with the legislature; and

(3)   It would not make much difference if legislative powers were reduced.

Supportive responses to these items indicate a willingness to maintain the legislative system in the face of generally unsatisfactory performance, and we can name it the "institutional commitment factor." As Table 3 shows, the compliance and institutional commitment factors are very clearly distinguishable for the mass public. Only one item has a secondary loading as high as .305, while all of the primary loadings are substantially higher.

The factor-analytic results with the data from the mass public are replicated for the party leaders sample, and, with one deviation in each case, for both attentive constituents and legislators. Only the lobbyists deviate substantially from the dominant factor pattern. While we cannot fully account for the erratic pattern of factor loadings for the 99 lobbyists in our analysis, we are satisfied that the evidence is sufficient to conclude that there are, indeed, two definable subdimensions of diffuse legislative support in our attitudinal data which deserve some separate consideration. In practice, however, we are mainly concerned with the principal component for the purpose of giving respondents a support score. We used the factor loadings in Table 3 to generate standardized factor scores for all respondents, and these scores become our exact measurement of diffuse legislative support for purposes of further analysis.

For the sake of simplicity of presentation, we have divided all respondents into one of three categories—those whose legislative support scores are High, those whose scores are Medium, and those whose scores are Low. In the High category are those whose support scores fall one-half of a standard deviation above the mean; Medium scorers are from one-half a standard deviation above the mean to one-half a standard deviation below the mean; and, Low supporters were one-half a standard deviation below the mean. Thusly dividing the support scores into three groups makes possible the straightforward comparison of our five groups in terms of their relative levels of diffuse legislative support (shown in Table 4). Examination of the percentages for each group makes the sizeable differences among them fairly clear. High support shifts from 15% in the mass public, to nearly half among lobbyists and attentive constituents, to

Table 4 Diffuse Legislative Support in the Mass
Public and Among Political Elites

Diffuse Legislative Support (Principal Component)	Mass Public	Leaders	Attentive Constituents	Lobbyists	Legislators
High	15.2	39.6	49.8	45.5	63.5
Medium	32.0	31.9	29.8	38.4	23.8
Low	52.8	28.6	20.5	16.2	12.7
Total	100.0	100.1	100.1	100.1	100.0
No. of cases	1,001	90	484	99	181

about two-thirds among legislators. Low support moves in the opposite direction.

If we use the statistical method of analysis of variance to assess inter-group differences in support, we find evidence of very substantial differences in support among the five groups of respondents ($F = 124.36$, $df = 4,1831$, p .001). When the separate factors of compliance and institutional commitment are utilized to compare these groups, group differences hold. In addition, to make the shape of diffuse legislative support across our groups of respondents crystal clear, we can plot the mean support scores for each group, showing the principal component means and means for each of the separate factors. Figure 1 displays these comparisons, and shows in a very graphic form the extent to which legislative support climbs from the mass public to legislators. Insofar as the principal factor is concerned, the largest difference between groups of respondents occurs between the mass public and the elite groups (t-test differences are all significant at the .05 level or higher). At the same time, legislators differ significantly in support from the other three elite groups—they are more supportive of the legislature than lobbyists, party leaders, or attentive constituents. The figure indicates that the significantly higher legislative support exhibited by legislators is mainly due to their much higher level of institutional commitment (Factor II). All the elite groups differ significantly from the mass public on the compliance factor (Factor I), but do not differ from one another. However, in the case of institutional commitment, all of the elite groups are significantly more supportive than the mass public, and legislators are significantly more supportive than other elite groups. These results are as they should be—we would have no particular reason to expect legislators to be more compliant than other groups of political leaders, but it is quite plausible that they, as members of the

Figure 1 Mean Diffuse Legislative Support Levels

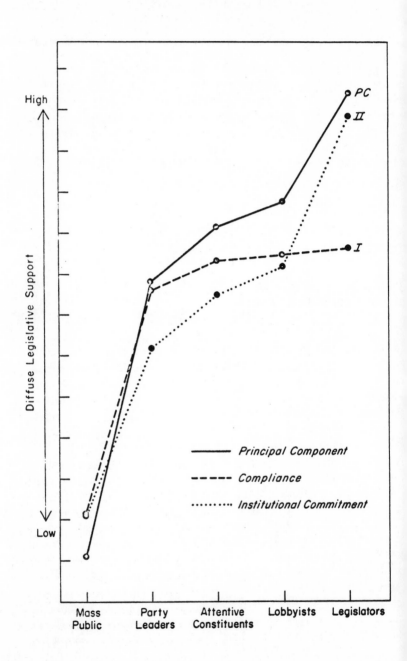

institution, should be more committed to it than members of elite groups outside the institution.

It should be pointed out that legislative support in the mass public is quite high. In Table 4 and Figure 1, support in the mass public is shown to be low in relation to political elite groups. But this should not imply in any sense that the mass of citizens do not support the legislature and political elites do support it. In fact, we would expect analyses to demonstrate that, relative to mass publics in other political systems, support for the legislature in Iowa is high. In general, Iowa is a supportive political environment for the legislature. But we have shown that legislative support grows very dramatically as one goes from the mass public to county party leaders, to attentive constituents, to lobbyists, and to legislators.

COMPARISON OF SPECIFIC AND DIFFUSE SUPPORT

It may be thought that specific and diffuse legislative support are essentially the same things. We certainly would expect them to have some relationship to one another. It would be surprising if those whose diffuse support for the legislature is high were not at least somewhat more inclined to evaluate the legislature more favorably than low diffuse supporters. At the same time, specific and diffuse support are conceptually distinct, and our measurements of them are independent. Direct comparisons between the two are shown in Table 5. Here we have, in effect, combined the data in Tables 1 and 4. In order to make the presentation more readable, and

Table 5 Comparisons of Specific and Diffuse
Legislative Support

Group	Specific Legislative Support	Diffuse Legislative Support		
		High	Medium	Low
Mass Public	High	60.1	55.9	52.7
	Low	39.9	44.1	47.4
	Total	100.0	100.0	100.1
Party Leaders	High	65.7	48.2	53.8
	Low	34.3	51.7	46.2
	Total	100.0	99.9	100.0
Attentive Constituents	High	62.6	58.4	47.5
	Low	37.4	41.6	52.5
	Total	100.0	100.0	100.0
Lobbyists	High	76.7	63.6	50.0
	Low	23.3	32.4	50.0
	Total	100.0	100.0	100.0

without doing injustice to the results, we have combined those who rated the legislature as doing an excellent job or good job into the category "high," and we have labeled as "low" those who rated the legislature as doing a fair job or a poor job. Inspection of Table 5 indicates that there is, indeed, some relation between diffuse and specific legislative support. In every group, a greater proportion of those whose diffuse support is high give the legislature a higher rating than do low diffuse supporters. For instance, in the mass public 60% of the high diffuse supporters evaluated the legislature as doing an excellent or good job, while only 53% of the low diffuse supporters gave the legislature those ratings, and this pattern is consistent for the other groups as well. We cannot include legislators in this comparison because we did not ask them to evaluate themselves, so we do not have specific support data from them.

At the same time, it is clear from Table 5 that the relationship between diffuse and specific support is not a strong one. Except for lobbyists, more than a third of the high diffuse supporters in each group give the legislature a low evaluation; and, roughly half of the low diffuse supporters in every category are high in specific support. To make the case another way, we could compare those who are high or low in specific support to see if diffuse support varied. Doing so produces the same conclusion. There is not a very significant difference between those who evaluate the legislature highly or poorly in terms of variations in diffuse support. We conclude that the relation between specific and diffuse support is positive but fairly weak, and that the two are quite distinctive types of legislative support.

Another way to get at differences between the two types of legislative support is to look at the effect of party identification on them. We would expect party identification to have some effect upon evaluation of the performance of a particular session of the legislature. If the legislature were controlled by the Democrats, as was the case in Iowa in 1965, we would anticipate that Democratic party identifiers would give the legislature a higher rating than Republicans. If the legislature were controlled by the Republicans, as the lower house was in 1967 in Iowa, we would expect the reverse. But diffuse support for the legislature—support for it as an institution—should not be affected by differences in party identification.

We have not probed these possibilities in great depth, controlling comparisons between party identification and both diffuse and specific support for a host of potentially relevant variables which may influence these particular inter-relationships. We are satisfied that the bivariate comparisons provide sufficient evidence, however, that the effect of party identification on support works the way we have suggested. As

Specific Legislative Support	Party Identification				
	Strong Democrat	Weak Democrat	Independent	Weak Republican	Strong Republican
High	64.3	58.4	55.5	53.0	45.7
Low	35.8	41.7	44.5	47.1	54.3
Total	100.1	100.1	100.0	100.1	100.0
No. of cases	179	168	191	168	197

Table 6 shows, for example, there is a modest relationship between party identification and evaluation of the legislature. This table presents the results only for the mass public, but it is sufficient illustration. For the mass public, who were interviewed following the Democratic-controlled 1965 legislative session, Democratic identifiers gave the legislature a higher rating than did Republican identifiers. If we look at similar tables for the elite respondents, especially for party leaders and attentive constituents, we find that, since they were interviewed after the 1967 session in which the Republicans dominated one house and were a very large minority in the other, Republican identifiers tended to rate the legislature more favorably than Democrats.

The effect of party identification on diffuse legislative support is a different matter. Here we do not find a significant relationship between the two. Again, Table 7 shows these variables for the mass public sample. Inspection of the table suggests relatively small differences among the categories of party identifiers. What is more, if anything Republicans exhibit higher support than Democrats, whereas the reverse was indicated in the case of specific support: 15% of the Strong Democrats were in the high diffuse support category, compared to 21% of the Strong Republicans. And, essentially the same results as those presented in Table 7 are observed for the elite respondents. Differences in party identification do affect specific support measurably more than they affect diffuse support.

We can assess these relationships in a more rigorous way by examining the statistical tests for differences as party identification may or may not influence legislative support. For instance, the relationship between party identification and specific legislative support for the mass public produces a chi-square significant at the .01 level, while in the same terms the relationship between party identification and diffuse legislative support

Table 7 Diffuse Support for the Legislature and Party
Identification in the Mass Public

Diffuse Legislative Support	Party Identification				
	Strong Democrat	Weak Democrat	Independent	Weak Republican	Strong Republican
High	15.0	11.1	16.5	12.8	20.8
Medium	33.2	26.8	33.5	31.3	32.4
Low	51.9	62.1	50.0	55.9	46.9
Total	100.1	100.0	100.0	100.0	100.1
No. of cases	187	190	200	179	207

is not statistically significant. Similarly, t-test differences between strong party identifiers show a significant difference between Strong Democrats and Strong Republicans in the mass public ($p < .01$) for specific support, but in the case of diffuse legislative support the difference between strong identifiers is not significant. However, even in the case of the relation between party identification and specific support, it should be pointed out that the strength of the relationship is not very great for any group (judging from tau-C's or gamma's). For specific support, there is a positive relation with party identification in the mass public, and a moderately negative relation in the elite samples, and the relationships between party identification and specific support are consistently stronger in all groups than is the case for diffuse support. So, we are prepared to conclude that specific and diffuse legislative support are distinctive in the sense that the former is affected to some extent by party identification and the latter is hardly affected at all by it.

We do not plan to consider the phenomenon of specific legislative support further. We have measured it only tentatively, and our interest is actually in the more underlying phenomenon of diffuse legislative support. Furthermore, we are now justified, we think, in dropping consideration of party identification as an important independent variable, since it has an insignificant bivariate relationship to diffuse support. We are saying that party differences may be important in accounting for variations in the immediate performance evaluation of legislatures, but partisan identification does not appear to be very important in an explanation of variations in diffuse support for legislature as an institution.

We now move to an analysis of the perceptions and expectations about the legislature held by the public and elite groups, and their attitudes toward the way in which the legislature works. Specifically, we will examine the relation to diffuse legislative support of:

(1)   the perceptions and expectations citizens and leaders have in regard to the kinds of people who serve as legislators;

(2)   the motives citizens and leaders attribute to legislators for running for public office; and

(3)   the attitudes citizens and leaders have toward the representativeness of the legislature and the use of compromise in legislative decision-making.

We expect these factors to bear some positive relationship to legislative support.

III. LEGISLATORS' ATTRIBUTES

PERSPECTIVES OF CITIZENS AND LEADERS

What kind of a person should a legislator be in the minds of his constituents? What do constituents think legislators are like? In order to deal with these questions, we asked respondents in our public and elite samples to evaluate a set of twenty attributes which have variously been suggested as characteristics of legislators. These twenty attributes are listed in Table 8. All of our respondents were asked first to indicate to what extent they thought legislators ought to have each attribute, ranking them on a scale from 1 (very important to have the attribute in question) to 4 (not at all important). Then, respondents were asked to make judgments about roughly what proportion of the members of the legislature actually had each attribute, gauging them on a scale from 1 (all members) to 5 (none of the members). By giving each respondent a score of one to four points for responses to the first set of rankings, and scoring respondents from one to five on the second set, it is possible to see what kinds of priorities are given in the general public and among leadership groups to different kinds of legislator-attributes. These mean raw scores are shown in Table 8 for the general population sample.

The ordering of legislator-attributes by the general public presents some interesting variations between characteristics citizens think legislators ought to have and those they think actually characterize the legislature (Nix, McIntyre and Dudley, 1968: 423-432). As a group, respondents in the Iowa sample ranked attributes of good character, knowledge and ability, and social status highest, and they ranked attributes of personal

Table 8   Means and Ranks of Scores for Characteristics of
Legislators in the Public Sample (N = 1,001)

Characteristics of Legislators	Important for Legislators to Have the Characteristic		Extent to Which Legislators Actually Have Characteristic	
	Mean	Rank	Mean	Rank
Completely honest	1.08	1	2.50	10
Study problems thoroughly	1.18	2	2.36	8
Know will of people of district	1.27	3	2.31	7
Hard working	1.30	4	2.30	6
Interested in serving others	1.32	5	2.26	5
Special knowledge about state government	1.46	6	2.40	9
Friendly toward others	1.51	7	2.14	2
High prestige in community	1.64	8	2.17	4
Influential in own district	1.64	9	2.16	3
Concerned with small details	1.97	10	3.01	17
Trained in legal work	2.01	11	2.84	15
Just an average citizen	2.09	12	2.51	11
Loyal to his political party	2.14	13	2.06	1
College graduate	2.46	14	2.66	12
Change things slowly if at all	2.51	15	3.10	18
Held previous office	2.55	16	2.69	14
Between ages 45-55	2.78	17	2.68	13
Political beliefs that don't change	2.92	18	2.85	16
Only interested in re-election	3.58	19	3.35	19
Seek personal gain or profit	3.64	20	3.54	20

99322

gain or manipulation lowest. When the rank orders for attributes of legislators are compared to ranks for characteristics they should have, some rather dramatic shifts occur.[3] While being completely honest ranks first as a trait legislators should have, it drops to the median rank of attributes legislators are perceived to possess. The highest ranking for perceived attributes is for political party loyalty. On the other hand, citizens tend to regard legislators as more friendly, influential in their districts, and prestigious than they should be, in terms of ranked importance. At the same time, the two ranked orderings are highly intercorrelated ($r_s = .64$).

It is apparent that the items included in Table 8 could be grouped into several distinctive sets, and doing so helps to reduce the complexity of dealing with twenty different categories. More importantly, we want to be in a position to make fairly easy comparisons among our samples—the public, attentive constituents, party leaders, lobbyists, and legislators. It would be an excessively laborious presentation to display the raw rank orderings for all of these groups, so we have illustrated the major details of our analysis with the general population sample. With the data from that sample, we factor-analyzed both ratings of characteristics felt by respondents to actually characterize the legislature.[4] The factor analysis of legislator-attributes is displayed in Table 9; the factorial structure for actual perceived characteristics is so similar that we have not shown it. Six factors accounted for more than half of the variance in scores, and the factorial structure is quite unambiguous. We have added to the factor analysis presented in Table 9 the mean of the means of items from Table 8 included in each factor, and the rank order of factors based upon these means.

The highest ranking factor in terms of mean scores, Factor II, included items having to do with the purposive activity of legislators and is among the top two factors in accounting for variance explained. The second ranking factor, Factor IV, including honesty, knowledge of and influence in the legislative district, and community prestige, can be given the summary label the "community status" factor. The factor ranking third, Factor V, can be called the "slow and deliberate change" factor from the manifest character of the two items highly loaded on it. The fourth ranking factor in terms of means, Factor I, accounts for nearly one-third of the explained variance and deals with the experience or preparation of legislators. The party-loyalty factor, Factor VI, ranks fifth in mean scores, followed by self-motivation, Factor III. The factor analysis and mean scores for the twenty legislator-attributes rated by the general public respondents suggest, therefore, the following hierarchy of expectations about the characteristics of legislators:

Table 9   Factor Analysis of Characteristics Legislators Ought to Have in the Public Sample

Characteristics of Legislators	I	II	III	IV	V	VI	Means of Items Included in Factor	Rank of Importance of Factors
Experience Factor							2.45	4
Held previous office	.719							
Trained in legal work	.686							
College graduate	.583							
Between ages 45-55	.471					.336		
Purposive Activity Factor							1.32	1
Interested in serving others		.804						
Study problems thoroughly		.737						
Special knowledge of state gov't	.345	.713		-.340				
Hard working		.436						
Self-Motivation Factor							3.61	6
Seek personal gain or profit			.813					
Only interested in re-election			.755					
Community Status Factor							1.54	2
Influential in own district				-.653				
Know will of people in district	.333			-.637				
Completely honest		.323		-.552				
High prestige in community				-.513				
Slow and Deliberate Change Factor							2.24	3
Concerned with details					.804			
Change things slowly					.655			
Party Loyalty Factor							2.53	5
Political beliefs that don't change						.703		
Loyal to political party						.691		

24

(1) purposive activity;
(2) community status;
(3) slow and deliberate change;
(4) experience;
(5) party loyalty; and
(6) self-motivation.

A similar analysis was carried out for respondents' ratings of the twenty basic attributes in terms of whether legislators actually exhibited them. The rankings of similar factors for perceived actual attributes were:

(1) community status;
(2) purposive activity;
(3) party loyalty;
(4) experience;
(5) slow and deliberate change; and
(6) self-motivation.

This shift in the rankings of factors suggests the nature of differences between Iowans' expectations and perceptions of legislator attributes. The community status and purposive activity factors reverse positions; party loyalty exchanges places with slow and deliberate change; experience remains fourth in rank, and self-motivation is at the bottom of both rankings.

While these rankings of attribute factors in the general pubic are of considerable interest in themselves, we were anxious to move to comparisons between the public and elite groups. We do this very simply by calculating means of raw score means for the items in each attribute factor for each subsample. Comparison of these means and the rank order of factors for each sample group makes it possible to see in gross terms to what extent public and elite groups differ, and to what extent priorities for perceived and expected characteristics differ. We show these means and ranks in Table 10. The principal conclusion which can be drawn from Table 10 is the overwhelming agreement among elite groups, and by the general public, on the priorities which both are thought to characterize legislators and are expected of legislators. Political leaders differ in many respects from the public, as we have shown earlier. But, in respect to their perspectives on the qualities of legislators they are very much in agreement.

LEGISLATOR ATTRIBUTES AND SUPPORT

We now want to examine the connections between factors identifying varying types of perceptions and expectations of the attributes of

Table 10 Perceptions and Expectations of Attributes of Legislators: Mean of Means of Attribute Factors by Sub-Sample

Attribute Factors	Perceived Attributes										Expected Attributes									
	Public		Consti- tuents		Party Leaders		Lobbyists		Legis- lators		Public		Consti- tuents		Party Leaders		Lobbyists		Legis- lators	
	X̄	Rank	X̄	Rank	X̄	Rank	X̄	Rank	X̄	Rank	X̄	Rank	X̄	Rank	X̄	Rank	X̄	Rank	X̄	Rank
Experience	2.7	4	3.1	5	3.1	5	3.1	4	3.2	5	2.4	4	3.0	5	3.0	5	3.0	5	3.1	5
Purposive Activity	2.3	2	2.6	3	2.6	3	2.6	3	2.4	2	1.3	1	1.3	1	1.3	1	1.4	1	1.5	1
Self- Motivation	3.4	6	3.7	6	3.7	6	3.7	6	3.9	6	3.6	6	3.8	6	3.8	6	3.7	6	3.8	6
Community Status	2.2	1	2.3	1	2.2	1	2.2	1	2.2	1	1.5	2	1.4	2	1.4	2	1.5	2	1.6	2
Slow and Deliberate Change	3.1	5	3.0	4	3.0	4	3.2	5	3.1	4	2.2	3	2.5	3	2.4	3	2.6	3	2.6	3
Party Loyalty	2.5	3	2.4	2	2.4	2	2.6	2	2.7	3	2.5	5	2.8	4	2.5	4	2.8	4	2.8	4

legislators and diffuse legislative support. We can first examine each factor in relation to support. These relationships are most conveniently presented graphically, showing legislative support on one axis of a set of graphs, and the factors on the other axis. Six parts of such graphs will depict the nexus between attribute factors and support both for respondents' perceptions and their expectations. These graphs are presented in Figures 2 through 7. In these exhibits we have combined all of the elite groups together, since the picture is not significantly different when each leadership group is plotted separately and the graphs are much more readable in this more simplified form.

One general observation which can be made about these figures is that they illustrate again the hiatus between the general public and the elite groups in their general levels of legislative support. In every one of these displays, the elite groups are invariably higher in support than the public. Another general observation which is indicated by these figures, and registered in a variety of other ways in our evidence, is that, for the most part, neither public nor elite groups exhibit very great differences for each factor in the way in which perceptions of the legislature, and expectations about it, operate. While there are some perception-expectation differences, and as we shall see these differences can be of some importance, Iowans of all kinds are generally inclined to perceive the state legislature to approximate what they expect it to be.

On the Experience Factor, higher legislative support accrues to those in both the public and in elite groups who think that relatively few legislators have the attributes in the cluster than to those who perceive that many legislators have these attributes. Similarly, higher support is forthcoming among those who think these experience factors are important for legislators to have, than among those who *expect* legislators to have the experience characteristics. In more down-to-earth terms, this simply means, perhaps surprisingly, that to the extent citizens perceive or expect legislators to be experienced they are likely to be less supportive of the legislature. We certainly anticipated the opposite result, and it is not entirely clear why the present findings should occur. The only explanation we can offer is the seemingly widespread acceptance of the notion of the amateur legislator among Iowans—the part-time legislator, the amateur politician, the Jacksonian democratic man au natural is the folk hero of Iowa politics. These results may be a consequence of this set of generalized attitudes about politicians. Thus, those who support the legislature the most also tend to perceive legislators as amateurs and expect that this should be so.

With regard to Purposive Activity, Figure 3 makes it clear that public and leaders have some tendency to show lower legislative support if they perceive and expect the items in this cluster to be unimportant and

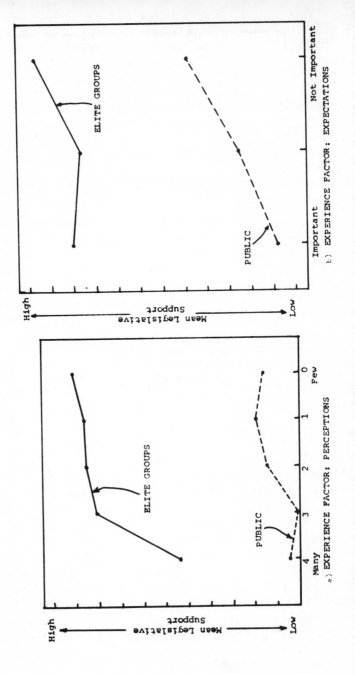

Figure 2   The Experience Factor and Legislative Support

Figure 3   The Purposive Activity Factor and Legislative Support

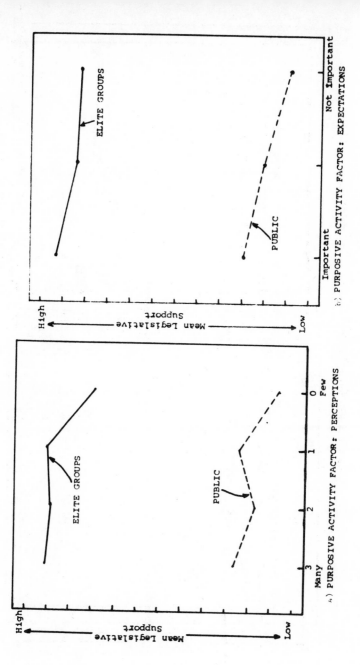

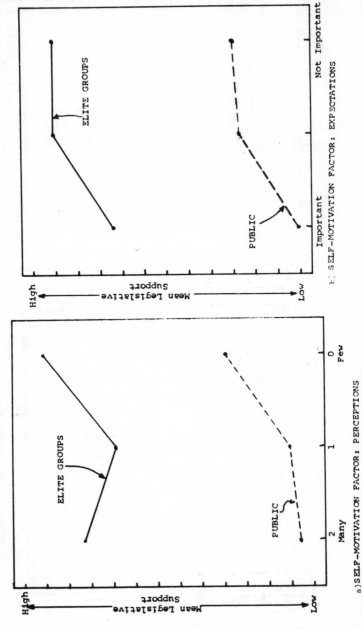

Figure 4 The Self-Motivation Factor and Legislative Support

a) SELF-MOTIVATION FACTOR: PERCEPTIONS

b) SELF-MOTIVATION FACTOR: EXPECTATIONS

Figure 5   The Community Status Factor and Legislative Support

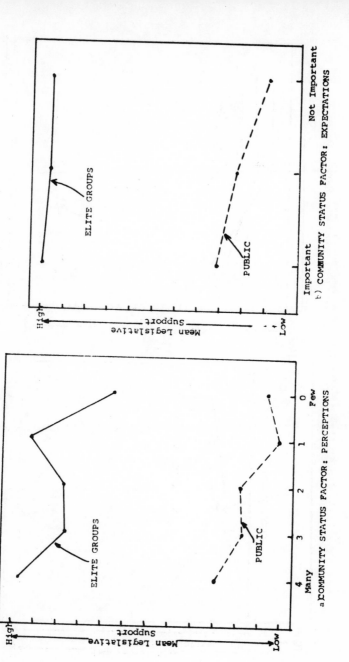

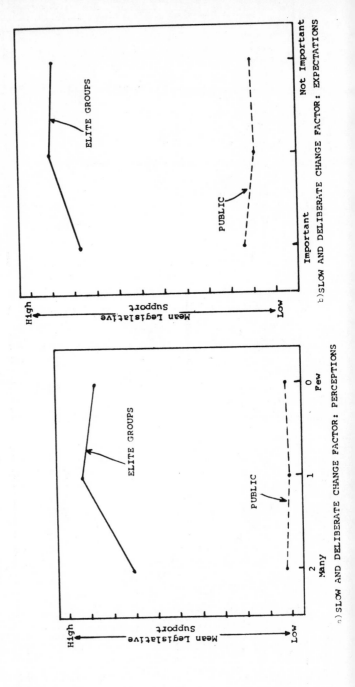

Figure 6   The Slow and Deliberate Change Factor and Legislative Support

32

Figure 7 The Party Loyalty Factor and Legislative Support

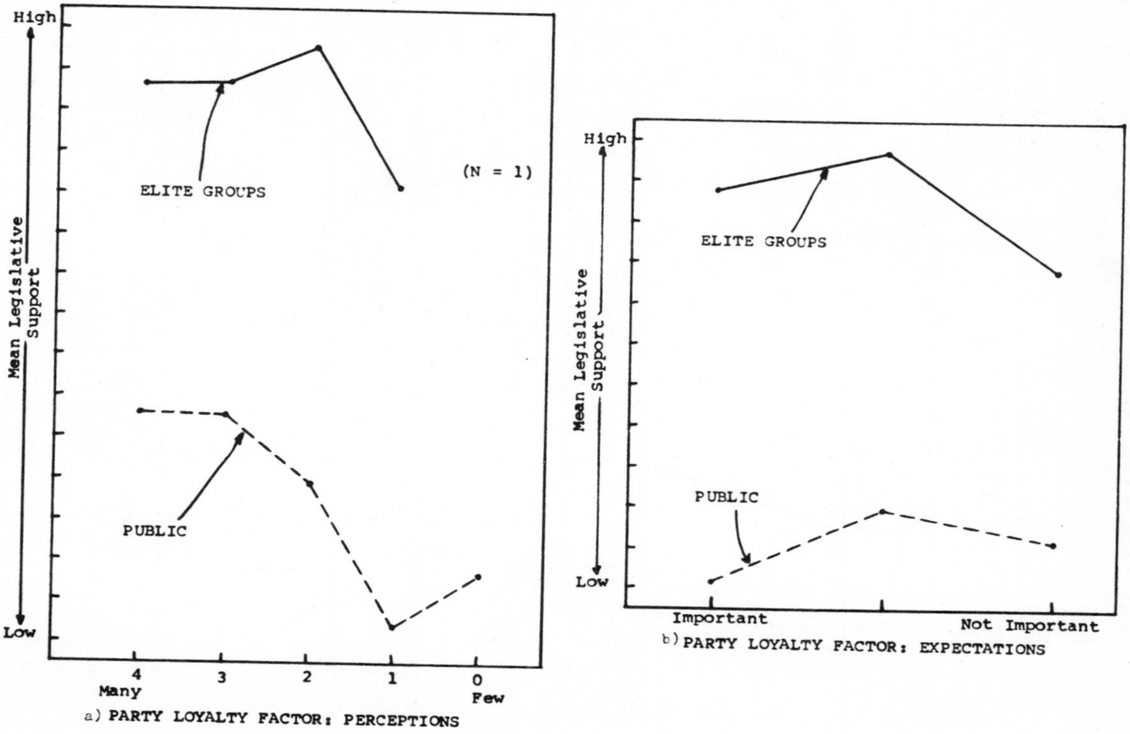

characterizing few legislators. Legislative support is relatively higher among those who both perceive and expect legislators to be interested in serving others, to study problems thoroughly, to have some special knowledge about state government, and to be hard-working. Conversely, there is some tendency for Self-Motivation, shown in Figure 4, to work the other way. It could easily have been supposed that high legislative supporters would tend to regard self-seeking as an unimportant characteristic for legislators to have, and to feel that relatively few legislators were only interested in their re-election and seeking and personal gain or profit.

Figure 5, which displays the Community Status Factor, presents some interesting results also. There is a tendency for high supporters among both public and elite groups to perceive legislators as having the community status characteristics—honesty, prestige, empathy, and influence. Among the general population, there is a moderately positive relationship between relative location in terms of the Community Status Factor and legislative support, although elite groups exhibit little difference from the mass public in this case. With respect to the Slow and Deliberate Change Factor, shown in Figure 6, elite groups show some slight tendency to change things slowly and be concerned with small details, but there are no substantial differences among the general citizenry on this count.

The pattern of results for the Party Loyalty Factor is not very easy to interpret, as a look at Figure 7 will suggest. Support is generally higher for those who think many legislators are loyal to their own political party, and support is lower among those who perceive few legislators are loyal to their party, but the relationship is not very regular. Expectations of party loyalty are less definitive; for the elite groups it is fairly clear that high legislative supporters expect party loyalty, but for the public the reverse is the case. And, it is consistent with a good deal of our evidence about party loyalty that public ambiguity is set against the orientations of the elite groups who emphasize the importance of the loyal partisan.

We have indicated that, while perceptions of the attributes of legislators and expectations about them are not greatly different in our Iowa samples, there are some gaps between them. To the extent that such perceptions and expectations are congruent, we would hypothesize that diffuse legislative support would be high; to the extent these are incongruent, we would expect legislative support to be low. To put it more simply, support should be lower for people for whom the legislature does not live up to expectations, and higher for those who expect legislators to have certain kinds of characteristics and perceive that they do have them. We have tested this hypothesis in considerable detail with the data from the general population sample, and for some of the attribute factors there is, indeed, a significant difference in legislative support in the expected direction between congruent and incongruent respondents with respect to perception-expectation differentials. These significant differences occur on the factors that show fairly strong correlations for legislative support with Community Status, Experience, and Self-Motivation. Considering the very high legislative support level in the Iowa sample, and the relatively meager number of respondents for whom there is any significant perception-expectation differential, we are fortunate to have found even some statistically significant differences between congruent and incongruent respondents in legislative support.

More relevant to the general line of argument in this inquiry is our analysis of the multiple effects of the attribute factors on support. We have performed a multiple regression analysis for each subsample, testing the joint effects of both perceptual and expectational attribute factors. The results of this analysis are shown in Table 11, where the multiple correlation (R) and the explained variance (R^2) are shown for each set of factor analyses and for each subsample. In general, the expectation factors together are more highly correlated with legislative support for all subsamples than are the perception factors. The expectation factors produce correlations of about .3 for each sample group, and account for about 10% of the variance in legislative support. The multiple correlations for the perception factors are very low, and account for only about 1% or less of the variance in support.

Table 11   Multiple Correlations Between Legislator Attribute Factors and Diffuse Legislative Support

Sub-Sample	Attributes Legislators Have (Perceptions)		Attributes Legislators Ought to Have (Expectations)	
	R	R^2	R	R^2
Public	.22	.05	.33	.11
Attentive Constituents	.13	.02	.25	.06
Party Leaders	.12	.02	.30	.09
Lobbyists	.24	.06	.31	.09
Legislators	.08	.01	.34	.12

IV. MOTIVATIONS FOR LEGISLATIVE CANDIDACY

A second set of perspectives on the legislator which we have sought to investigate has to do with attitudes toward the motivations of individuals who run for legislative office.[5] We expected support for the legislature to be, in part, a function of positive attitudes toward legislative candidacy. By positive attitudes, we mean simply attitudes consistent with general cultural norms about public office—that public office is a public trust, and that persons should seek public office out of a sense of civic duty and a desire to enact policies in the public interest, rather than seeking office for personal gain, out of a personal ambition or for special interests.

WHY LEGISLATORS RUN

In order to acquire data on motivations, at least of a rudimentary sort, we submitted a set of sixteen propositions about legislators' candidacy motivations to all of our respondents, asking them to indicate to what extent they thought each proposition properly characterized legislators as a group (did they think the attributed motive characterized all legislators, most, half, a few, or none?). Table 12 presents these propositions, mean scores for the public sample, and ranks of means. In the mass public, interest in politics was the reason for why legislators run attributed to most legislators (the mean 2.1 would lie between the categories "most" and "half"). Notice that motives involving personal and private aggrandizement, and motives involving pursuit of a particular issue, proposal, or policy, were attributed to the fewest legislators, and that some kind of political or civic obligation was thought to motivate legislative candidacies more often than private gain or special interest. It is also apparent that there is a great overlap among some of these attributed motives and that a number logically cluster together.

A standard factor analysis of inter-item correlations from the attributed motives in Table 12 produced five very manageable factors: a personal gain factor, a civic duty factor, a sociability factor, a political mobility factor, and a policy orientation factor. The items composing these factors, along with the major factor loadings, are shown in Table 13. Two of the sixteen items from Table 12 are not represented in Table 13 ("they are asked to run by party leaders" and "they are very interested in politics"), because they did not fit the most readily interpretable factor structure. Recruitment by party leaders is a separate factor, which we can consider in a somewhat different way later. Suffice it to say here that none of the groups of respondents separately differed in their perceptions of the extent of party leader recruitment, except for the group of legislators. On the average, the mass public and the nonlegislator elite groups perceived that more than half of the legislators were asked to run by party leaders, while legislators themselves perceived that fewer than half were party-recruited. The item "they are very interested in politics"

Table 12   Public Attitudes Concerning
Why Legislators Run

Attributed Motive	Mean*	Rank
They run because they are very interested in politics.	2.1	1
They run because this is a way to get ahead in politics.	2.4	2
They run because they are particularly concerned about issues before the legislature.	2.5	3
They run because they are asked to run by party leaders.	2.5	4
They run because they are politically ambitious.	2.6	5
They run because this is a stepping stone to a higher office.	2.6	6
They run because they feel that they ought to do it as good citizens.	2.7	7
They run because they feel an obligation to participate.	2.7	8
They run because it is a part of their duty as citizens.	2.8	9
They run because being in the legislature gives them contacts that are useful in other ways.	2.9	10
They run because they have some legislative proposals they want to push.	2.9	11
They run because they want to campaign for a special policy.	2.9	12
They run because it is a good way to make business contacts.	3.1	13
They run for personal gain or profit.	3.2	14
They run because they enjoy campaigning.	3.2	15
They run because they like to meet new people.	3.6	16

*These are ordered so that the high ranking ones indicate the motive is attributed to many legislators and the low ranking ones indicate the motive is attributed to a few. Item scoring was as follows: All = 1; Most = 2; Half = 3; Few = 4; and None = 5.

#Ranks are based upon unrounded means, which were not tied.

appears to hang limbo-like between the civic duty and sociability factors, and we are not sure why it does not attach itself securely to one or the other.

Having simplified perceptions of the motivational world of legislative recruitment into five major factors, we can make comparisons among sub-groups of respondents by factor-scoring them and comparing mean factor scores using analysis of variance. Since the raw mean factor scores for each factor by respondent group are not in themselves a particularly

Table 13 Factors Motivating Legislative Candidacies

Motivational Items	Factors*				
	I	II	III	IV	V
PERSONAL GAIN FACTOR					
Make contacts useful in other ways	.801				
Good way to make business contacts	.764				
Run for personal gain or profit	.718				
CIVIC DUTY FACTOR					
Part of duty as citizen		.801			
Feel an obligation to participate		.797			
Feel they ought to as good citizens		.779			
Particularly concerned about an issue		.540			
SOCIABILITY FACTOR					
Like to meet new people			.916		
Enjoy campaigning	.318	.375	.608		
POLITICAL MOBILITY FACTOR					
Politically ambitious				.863	
Way to get ahead in politics	.378			.703	
Stepping-stone to higher office	.443			.662	
POLICY ORIENTATION FACTOR					
Want to campaign for a special policy					.806
Have legislative proposal to promote					.790

*All factor loadings above .300 are shown.

meaningful number, we refrain from presenting the table of their values. It is more meaningful to concentrate on intergroup differences. These differences are shown in Table 14.

Lobbyists, party leaders, and attentive constituents did not differ significantly on any of the five factors. The mass public differed from at least one elite group on all of the factors, and from all elite groups on the political mobility and policy orientation factors. Across all groups, the greatest differences occurred on the political mobility factor, and the least occurred on the civic duty factor. With respect to motivations of personal gain, the mass public attributed this motive to more legislators

Table 14 Differences Among Groups in
Perceptions of Why Legislators Run

Factor	F	P	T-test differences where P $\angle$ .01
Personal Gain Factor	15.84	.01	Mass public differs from legislators, party leaders, and attentive constituents
Civic Duty Factor	4.28	N.S.	Legislators differ from mass public and attentive constituents
Sociability Factor	5.75	.05	Mass public differs from legislators and lobbyists; legislators differ from attentive constituents
Political Mobility Factor	99.09	.001	Mass public differs from all elite groups; legislators differ from lobbyists, party leaders, and attentive constituents
Policy Orientation Factor	13.37	.05	Mass public differs from all elite groups

than did legislators, party leaders, or attentive constituents. The mass public attributed reasons of civic duty to fewer legislative candidates than did legislators themselves, and so did attentive constituents, but legislators, lobbyists, and party leaders did not differ. On the sociability factor, the data suggest that citizens in general and attentive constituents thought significantly more legislators ran for sociability motives than did legislators, although legislators, lobbyists, and party leaders did not differ. In sum, the major differences in attributed motivations concerning why legislators run for office occurred between the mass public and the political elites. Attentive constituents lay closest to the mass public in these data, and lobbyists and party leaders differed from legislators only in their tendency to attribute political mobility motivations to legislators more than did legislators themselves.

The means for each sample groups on each of the candidacy motivation factors are given in Table 15. The rank orders of factors are also shown, although in some cases differences between factor means are very small, and they therefore must be interpreted very cautiously. It is interesting, however, that fairly sharp differences do materialize between the mass public and the elite groups. The most important reasons for legislative

Table 15 Attributed Candidacy Motivation Factors: Mean of Means of Factors by Sample

Motivation Factors	Public $\bar{X}$	Public Rank	Attentive Constituents $\bar{X}$	Attentive Constituents Rank	Party Leaders $\bar{X}$	Party Leaders Rank	Lobbyists $\bar{X}$	Lobbyists Rank	Legislators $\bar{X}$	Legislators Rank
Personal Gain	3.3	4	3.7	5	3.6	5	3.6	5	3.8	5
Civic Duty	2.9	2	2.9	1	2.8	1	2.9	1	2.7	1
Sociability	3.5	5	3.6	4	3.2	3	3.4	3	3.3	2
Political Mobility	2.6	1	3.3	2	3.1	2	3.3	2	3.5	3
Policy Orientation	3.2	3	3.5	3	3.6	4	3.6	4	3.6	4

candidacies given in the public are those involving political mobility. Citizens in general tend to think that the main reason legislators run for the office is because they are politically ambitious. While political mobility ranks highly among elite groups, too, the ranking factor for them is civic obligation. All groups, mass public and elites, consider personal gain to be the least important motivation for legislative candidacies.

At the same time, while there are small but interesting differences among sample groups, the clustering of means near the center of the scale suggests across all groups a very large range of consensus among them on candidacy motivation. It certainly would be stretching the evidence beyond credulity to suggest that there are vast differences suggested here between public and elites.

ATTITUDES TOWARD CANDIDACY AND LEGISLATIVE SUPPORT

We expected attitudes toward the motivations for legislative candidacies to bear some relation to supportive predispositions to the legislative institution. We thought those respondents who thought few legislators sought office purely for personal gain, to make business or political contacts, or for political mobility, and who believed that many legislators ran out of a sense of civic duty or to further specific policies, in our samples would be relatively more supportive of the legislature. We can analyze these expected relationships simply by making a calculation for each of our samples of the mean diffuse legislative-support scores in terms of the extent to which sets of respondents were "high" or "low" on our motivation factors. While these mean legislative-support scores, displayed in Table 16, are constructed scores which have no ready interpretation in themselves, they do allow one to see the relative effects of variable location of respondents on the motivation factors for legislative support.

The results of the analysis are not entirely as we had expected. Indeed, for most sample groups those who were high on the Personal Gain factor (that is, generally thought few legislators ran for personal gain) were relatively more supportive of the legislature than those who were low on this factor, although the relationship is not entirely regular for all elite groups and, in fact, slightly reversed for legislators themselves. The product-moment correlation between the Personal Gain factor and legislative support is $-.21$. The Civic Duty and Sociability factors proved to be uncorrelated with legislative support for all samples combined, although for legislators, support for the legislature was substantially higher among those who felt that many legislators ran out of a sense of civic duty than for those who believed that few members were so moti-

Table 16 Candidacy Motivation Factors and Diffuse Legislative Support

Factor by Sub-Sample	Mean Legislative Support Scores		
	Low on Motivation Factor	Intermediate on Motivation Factor	High on Motivation Factor
PERSONAL GAIN	Many run for Personal gain ⟵————————⟶		Few run for Personal gain
Public	-.42	-.43	-.22
Attentive Constituents	.36	.36	.49
Party Leaders	.29	.19	.32
Lobbyists	.48	.37	.54
Legislators	1.05	.70	.75
CIVIC DUTY	Few run for Civic Duty ⟵————————⟶		Many run for Civic Duty
Public	-.34	-.42	-.39
Attentive Constituents	.37	.40	.49
Party Leaders	.23	.56	.01
Lobbyists	.51	.40	.54
Legislators	.57	.66	.89
SOCIABILITY			
Public	-.37	-.39	-.41
Attentive Constituents	.48	.46	.28
Party Leaders	.50	.25	.26
Lobbyists	.81	.37	.39
Legislators	.90	.78	.60
POLITICAL MOBILITY	Few run for Political Mobility ⟵————————⟶		Many run for Political Mobility
Public	-.23	-.33	-.58
Attentive Constituents	.47	.49	.13
Party Leaders	.40	.24	.04
Lobbyists	.36	.64	.28
Legislators	.75	.74	.72
POLICY ORIENTATION	Many run for Policy ⟵————————⟶		Few run for Policy
Public	-.47	-.37	-.31
Attentive Constituents	.52	.32	.47
Party Leaders	.83	.22	.11
Lobbyists	.06	.51	.65
Legislators	.58	.96	.65

vated. In addition, although in the mass public legislative support did not vary in terms of the Sociability factor, in general for the elite groups support for the legislature was higher for those who felt that many legislators ran for sociability reasons than otherwise.

Our expectations about the effects of the Political Mobility factor on legislative support did not materialize very well. In fact, although we thought respondents would be more supportive if they believed that relatively few legislators ran out of motivations of political ambition, the reverse turned out to be the case for the mass public, attentive constituents, and party leaders. The results for lobbyists are inconclusive, and legislators did not differ in support levels across variations in the Political Mobility factor. The product-moment correlation for the entire data set proved to be positive ($r = +.25$). Similarly, sample groups differed in terms of their legislative support along the Policy Orientation factor. In the general public, our expectations were again not borne out; legislative support was, in fact, slightly higher (less negative) among those who believed that few legislators ran for purposes of promoting public policies. Interestingly enough, an even stronger relationship of this kind occurred among lobbyists. Lobbyists who thought few legislators ran for office for policy promotion reasons were much more supportive than those who felt that many legislators ran for this reason. Equally interesting are the results for party leaders, who, unlike lobbyists, are presumably concerned that legislators should be policy oriented. It turns out that our original expectations about the relationship between Policy Orientation and support were fulfilled only for party leaders. There is a pretty strong correlation for party leaders such that legislative support increases to the extent that party leaders believed legislators were motivated to be candidates for office by urges to promote policies. For the entire company of respondents, the correlation between the Policy Orientation factor and legislative support was $+.11$.

The combined effects of candidacy motivation factors on legislative support for each of our samples are not striking, although a modest proportion of the variance in legislative support is explained by these combined factors for lobbyists ($R^2 = .12$), who presumably are more sensitive in their daily work to the career motivations of legislators. The multiple correlations are shown in Table 17, along with the variance in legislative support explained by the combined candidacy motivation factors. The multiple correlations are in the vicinity of .2 for the general public, attentive constituents and legislators, .3 for party leaders, and .4 for lobbyists.

V. LEGISLATIVE REPRESENTATION

LEGISLATIVE REPRESENTATIVENESS AND COMPROMISE

We sought to take into account in our analysis of legislative support an additional feature of the perspectives of the represented: their attitudes toward the representativeness of the legislature, and toward legislative compromise. We asked all of our respondents attitude questions through which we hoped to assess their sense of representative efficacy—to what

Table 17 Attributed Candidacy Motivation Factors and
Legislative Support: Multiple Regression

Sample	Multiple Correlation and Variance Explained	
	R	R^2
Public	.23	.05
Attentive Constituents	.22	.05
Party Leaders	.29	.08
Lobbyists	.35	.12
Legislators	.15	.02

extent they thought the legislature represented its constituency well, and to what extent they thought the legislature was run by an oligarchy unconcerned with the public weal. We thought respondents who deemed the representativeness of the legislature very efficacious would exhibit considerably higher support for the institution as such than those who could agree that the legislature was unrepresentative of the citizenry. In addition, we sought to get some notion of respondents' views about legislative compromise, the sine qua non of legislative life. We thought support for the legislature would be higher among those who appeared to believe in legislative compromise than among those who seemed to scorn the accommodatory role of the legislature.

In order to gather some evidence on these matters, we asked all of our Iowa respondents a number of questions about their attitudes toward the representativeness of the legislature and the virtue of compromise. These items are listed in Table 18, along with the percentages of each sample group who agreed with each attitude statement. Between 25 and 29% of all sample groups except legislators indicated that they felt the legislature did not represent citizens very well; only 15% of the legislators themselves took this view. One-fourth of the respondents in the mass public indicated they felt the legislature was controlled by a clique unresponsive to public demands, but less than a fifth of the attentive constituents, party leaders and lobbyists took this view and only 8% of the legislators said so. Overwhelming majorities of all sample groups, however, indicated that the legislature usually acted in the public interest, and only a small proportion in each group suggested that the legislature need not pay attention to small opposition groups. Similarly, very high proportions in every sample appeared to endorse compromise and the accommodation of conflicting interests in the legislative arena.

Table 18 Attitudes Toward Representation and Compromise

Item	Percent Who Agree					
	Public	Attentive Constituents	Party Leaders	Lobbyists	Legislators	
The Iowa state legislature does not represent the citizens of Iowa very well.	28.5	27.1	25.6	25.3	15.4	
The legislature is controlled by a small handful of men who run it pretty much to suit themselves, no matter what the people want.	24.6	19.8	13.3	15.2	8.3	
Most of the things the legislature does are in the interest of the general public, rather than in the interests of special groups.	68.0	75.9	75.6	73.7	85.0	
The legislature need not pay attention to opposition to legislation if it comes from a rather small group.	8.5	5.6	3.3	4.0	4.9	
The state legislature is important because it is here that the differences of opinion about what the state ought to do can be compromised for the good of all	86.5	95.7	95.6	95.9	94.4	
When there is a sharp division of opinion in the legislature, both sides should try to go along with the interests of the other group as much as possible rather than insisting that their proposal is the only correct one.	69.2	72.1	74.4	66.7	64.1	

In keeping with our now familiar and standard analytical practice, we factor-analyzed these items, and the factor analysis produced results that would have been expected. The straightforward results of the factor analysis are presented in Table 19, where the evidence plainly shows two quite unambiguous factors: Representativeness and Compromise. Again, these factor loadings were used to score respondents on these two dimensions to create summary variables easily relatable to legislative support.

REPRESENTATIVENESS, COMPROMISE AND SUPPORT

Again in accord with our standard procedure, we divided respondents in each sample into high, intermediate and low clusters along the representativeness and compromise dimensions, and then calculated mean legislative-support scores for each of these clusters. For the Representativeness factor, we expected legislative support to be much higher among those whose representative efficacy was high and whose sentiments toward compromise were favorable. The means are shown in Table 20, where the expected relationship materializes for each sample group. For the mass public, the highly efficacious group with respect to representativeness had a slightly positive mean legislative-support score, while the low group was very low in legislative support. This same pattern, with varying degrees of strength, holds for each elite group, somewhat more strongly for party leaders and lobbyists than for attentive constituents and legislators. For all respondents taken together, the correlation between representativeness and legislative support is +.33.

We performed a similar kind of analysis for the conjunction between variation in respondent scores on the Compromise factor and legislative support. The relationship between attitudes toward compromise and support for the legislature is as we expected; there is a positive association in general between acceptance of compromise and legislative support. The mean legislative support scores by Compromise factor groups and sample groups are presented in Table 21. The relationship is quite marked for the public, lobbyists and legislators, where legislative support systematically goes down from the high-compromise to the low-compromise groups. For attentive constituents and party leaders the relationship is less regular, but still visible. Again putting all respondents together into one large data set, the correlation between variation in the Compromise factor and variation in legislative support is +.27.

Once again we combine factorial dimensions to assess their joint impact on legislative support. We do this for each sample group, calculating the multiple correlation coefficients and the variance explained by the combined dimensions. These coefficients are shown in Table 22. It

Table 19   Factor Analysis of Representation and
Compromise For the General Public
(N = 1,001)

Items	Factors*	
	I	II
REPRESENTATIVENESS		
State legislature does not represent citizens	.642	
Legislature controlled by handful	.707	
Legislature works for special interest	-.620	
Legislature can ignore small opposition	.412	
COMPROMISE		
Legislature compromises differences for the good of all		-.754
Both sides should go along with other groups as much as possible		.589

*All loadings above .300 are shown.

is clear that, for each sample except that of party leaders, the combined in-fluences of Representativeness and Compromise are at least somewhat more useful in accounting for variance in legislative support than either one of the two individually. In fact, the detailed differences in the explanatory power of the combined dimensions among sample groups are not manifestly explainable. We cannot advance an argument that helps to account for the fact that very little variance in legislative support is explained by these factors for party leaders, or for the fact that a relatively extraordinary proportion of the variance in legislative support is accounted for by these two dimensions for lobbyists. We can only suggest the possibility that the role of the party leader may be such as to debase the connection between

Table 20 Legislative Representativeness and Diffuse Legislative Support

Sample	Mean Legislative Support Scores		
	High Represen-tativeness	Intermediate Represen-tativeness	Low Represen-tativeness
Public	.011	-.376	-.658
Attentive Constituents	.963	.259	.206
Party Leaders	.518	.207	.063
Lobbyists	.984	.287	.073
Legislators	.935	.474	.436

Table 21 Legislative Compromise and Diffuse Legislative Support

Sample	Mean Legislative Support Scores		
	High Compromise	Intermediate Compromise	Low Compromise
Public	.231	-.436	-.564
Attentive Constituents	.724	.303	.329
Party Leaders	.596	.132	.206
Lobbyists	.873	.371	.101
Legislators	1.135	.653	.432

Table 22 Multiple Correlations Between Representation-Compromise and Diffuse Legislative Support

Sample	R	R^2
Public	.39	.16
Attentive Constituents	.34	.11
Party Leaders	.25	.06
Lobbyists	.54	.30
Legislators	.42	.17

representativeness-compromise and support for the legislature. There may be some tendency for party leaders to think of a supportable legislative institution as one in which party oppositions are maximized over inter-party accommodation, or who think the legislature ought to be run by a small group—the party leadership—in its own interest. For lobbyists the tendency to regard the legislature as a representative body in accord with politico-cultural norms, and as a compromising institution, may also be built into the lobbyists' role. Unlike the party militant, the lobbyist presumably is more likely to have a vested interest in legislative compromise and an occupational proclivity to think of the legislative body as a relatively adequate vehicle for the representation of the people.

VI. ANALYSIS OF COMBINED VARIABLES

How much of the variation in diffuse legislative support can be accounted for by the variables which we have considered in this analysis? We have dealt with some 23 variables in this inquiry, an unseemly number of variables to include in a multiple regression analysis.[6]

We have tried to reduce the number of variables to be included in an analysis of their multiple effects by making additive combinations of some of them. We have combined the two Experience attribute factors into one variable which measures both the importance respondents attribute to the set of legislator-characteristics and the extent to which respondents think legislators ought to be characterized by them. We have combined the two Self-Motivation attribute factors and the Personal Gain motivation factor into a composite variable which we will call Political Opportunism. This variable measures the extent to which respondents both perceived and expected legislators to seek personal gain and to be interested only in their reelection, and the extent to which making contacts for personal or business contacts was attributed to legislators as a motivation for seeking office. Finally, we combined the Purposive Activity and Community Status attribute factors together with the Civic Duty motivation factor to create a variable we have called "good-guys," since it arrays respondents in terms of the extent to which they think legislators are or should be more-or-less knowledgeable, hard-working, interested in public service, honest, in tune with sentiments in their districts, and prestigious and influential in their districts, along with the extent to which they think legislators are motivated to run for office out of a sense of civic duty. These operations reduced the total number of variables to 18, and, on the basis of these variables we conducted a step-wise multiple regression analysis against legislative support. This analysis makes it very clear that 5 of the 18 variables considered provide the bulk of the explanatory power: the Experience factors, the Representativeness factor, the Compromise factor, the Political Opportunism factors, and the Political Mobility factor. These five variables were, in the total sample, moderately correlated with legislative support when taken individually (the zero-order correlations are shown in Table 23). All together, they produced a multiple correlation coefficient of .56, and accounted for 31% of the variance in legislative support. Adding additional variables contributed very little to the multiple correlation or the variance explained. We can explain about a third of the variation in legislative support by taking into account the Experience factors, the Representativeness factor, the Compromise factor, and Political Opportunism factors, and the Political Mobility factor. And, the Experience, Representativeness, and Compromise variables are, of these the most important, judging from the standardized regression coefficients (shown in Table 23). When the regression analysis is put into the form of an equation indicating the character of the regression slopes, the best equation for these data is

$$X_1 = .36 + .13X_2 + .28X_3 + .23X_4 + .10X_5 - .13X_6$$

where

X_1 = legislative support
X_2 = experience factors
X_3 = representativeness factor
X_4 = compromise factor
X_5 = political opportunism factors
X_6 = political mobility factor

Table 23   Perspectives on the Legislature and Legislative
Support: Multiple Effects

Variables in the Regression Analysis	Zero-order Correlation with Legislative Support	Standardized Regression Coefficients (beta's)
Experience factors	.35	.26
Representativeness factor	.33	.27
Compromise factor	.26	.24
Political Opportunism Factors	.21	.14
Political Mobility factor	-.25	-.14

50

This equation simply indicates the preeminence in accounting for support for the legislature of expectations about the maturity, educational experience, and experience in public offices of legislators, attitudes toward the representativeness of the legislative institution, and attitudes toward making political compromises in the legislature. Notably missing from this explanatory system is the Party Loyalty attribute factor. Just as we found earlier that the partisan attachments of our respondents was not importantly associated with their degree of diffuse support for the legislature, we now see that expectations about the party loyalty of legislators do not make a significant contribution to legislative support. What we have shown, in the end, is that how citizens view the legislator, how they conceive of their relationship to the legislature, and how they perceive the way the legislature carries on its work, are factors which, in the specific ways in which we have delineated them, account for a substantial part of the degree of support citizens accord to the legislative institution.

VII. COMPARATIVE RESEARCH IMPLICATIONS

We have argued that the ways in which citizens view the legislature and the legislative process impinge quite heavily upon their supportive orientations toward the legislative institution. In pursuing this argument empirically, we have demonstrated that, over all, about a third of the variance in diffuse legislative support can be accounted for in terms of variables associated with the orientations of citizens and leaders to legislators' attributes, to motivations for candidacy, and to representativeness and compromise. In the analysis, we have made systematic comparisons between those in the general citizenry and important categories of political leaders. While we have demonstrated uniform differences between the aggregate levels of diffuse legislative support in the mass public and among political leaders, our investigation suggested that essentially the same explanatory strategy was appropriate for both citizens and leaders in accounting for variations in supportive orientations. In other of our reports of research findings from the analysis of our data we have mapped out the consequences of other sets of variables for variations in legislative support (see especially Boynton, Patterson and Hedlund, 1968: 163-173). Our work with the entire data set has made it possible to weigh the factors developed in this report along with other variables, such as extent of social and political stratification and elite status. Although this exploratory work has necessarily involved the consideration of a very large number of independent variables, which makes their analysis very unwieldy, we have been able to make estimates of the independent effects upon legislative support of several sets of independent variables, including the factors reported here and others. This summary analysis is far too detailed and complex to present here, but it probably is important to emphasize that we are able to demonstrate that the factors analyzed in this analysis are sustained as having independent effects upon diffuse support when factors we have developed in other papers, and additional ones, too, are taken into account.

Cross-sectional investigations in one subnational system clearly have great advantages. It has been possible for us to include samples from several relevant population strata, and to explore the effects of a large number of variables, in the kind of inquiry in depth that a single, cross-sectional investigation permits. But this kind of mapping operation has its limitations. Our particular research site is one which we assume is characterized by relatively high levels of regime support (Iowans hardly seem to be on the brink of revolt; they give appearance of being a very allegiant sample). Yet, without comparative research, we cannot tell systematically how the aggregate levels of legislative support in this one subnational system compare with others. What is more, we would like to know if the set of explanatory factors we have been able to develop in the Iowa research site works, or how it can be elaborated, in other research contexts. In fact, we have gathered data in thirteen other American states which permit us to construct most of our key variables in comparative terms, and take variables into account which could not appropriately be included in the Iowa data set (for instance, we could not analyze the effects of race in Iowa because the nonwhite population is miniscule). Although this extension of our research is of great interest, its presentation is a major research report in its own right. Suffice it to say here that our general analytical posture holds up very well in this kind of comparative analysis, although the cross-state comparisons suggest interesting interstate differences and provide opportunities for analyses of independent variables which could not be analyzed effectively with the Iowa samples (such as race or urbanization at the individual level, or system-level properties such as party competition, malapportionment, levels of legislative conflict, or levels of political participation; see Patterson, Wahlke, and Boynton, 1973: 302-307).

Although we have been very profoundly pressed to submit our own research instruments and analytical strategy to comparative treatment, the analysis with the Iowa samples provides the kind of mapping which fruitfully precedes cross-system comparisons. When our work began, we were not sure we could develop adequate measures of the dependent variable, and our search for useful independent variables was largely exploratory. Our limited comparative work in the American subnational context indicates that, at least within one national polity, comparisons are both analytically rewarding and theoretically essential.

But our research design has been fulfilled, and our decisions regarding conceptualization, measurement, and analysis have come home to roost. What about future comparative research on supportive orientations toward legislative institutions, even cross-national inquiry? What lessons, if any, have been learned from this extensive research in a single American state, and the modest cross-state comparisons, for comparative research on legislative support?

One conceptual contribution our work has made concerns the distinction between specific and diffuse support. We have been able to show that these two elements of support are more than simply conceptually distinct elements—as we have measured them they are empirically distinct elements. We take our results to indicate that Easton's differentiation of specific and diffuse support should be retained in comparative research. While we recognize that precipitous degeneration of specific support for the legislature (in terms of performance evaluation) might ultimately contribute to erosion of diffuse support for the legislative institution, we think this effect entails empirical inquiry in which specific and diffuse support must be kept analytically distinct. While we have, in our own work, concentrated our efforts on the measurement and analysis of diffuse legislative support, we believe that attention to specific support should be retained in comparative research. At this stage, we know too little about the relationship between the two to abandon attempts to gather data on one or the other. In systems at an early phase of political development, for instance, it is possible that specific support is the critical factor. Citizens in less developed systems may first acquire attachment to the regime by virtue of their positive orientations toward legislative (and other governmental) performance, or through their trust in and support for the authorities (e.g., the members of the legislature). And, in highly developed systems, with highly legitimate legislative institutions, we need to remain open to new findings about the reciprocal effects of specific and diffuse support.

With regard to the empirical measurement of diffuse legislative support (or, for that matter, for the general conception of support), we constructed measurement items on the basis of a conceptualization which included both the notions of legislative commitment and compliance. Accordingly, our measurement of legislative support exhibits two identifiable dimensions. Two things can be said about our measurement of diffuse legislative support. First, the test items, though conceptually grounded, clearly require further and more careful validation. Second, we are inclined to feel that, in comparative research, measurement of diffuse support should concentrate on the factor of legislative commitment. While the compliance items used in the Iowa study provided an adequate and elegant handle on the measurement of diffuse support for the legislature in that context, retention of the compliance dimension in comparative studies might produce inappropriate results. This is especially true in view of the conceptual reality that acts of compliance or compliant attitudes may indicate support, but noncompliance may not necessarily constitute evidence of lack of support for the legislative institution.

Again, our work focused upon support for the legislature among citizens and leaders. In the Iowa study, it has been reasonable to assume that public support for the legislature would enhance the capacity of the legislature to legitimize the state political regime as a whole, or to confer legitimate authority on other governmental actors and agencies (e.g., the governor). However, in comparative research, especially in less developed systems, greater empirical attention probably should be given to the role of the legislature itself in contributing to support or lack of it for the regime as a whole. In research with this kind of focus, specific or diffuse support for the legislature would be taken as fostering or inhibiting the capability of the legislature to construct support for the regime.

Finally, although our research recognized the importance of differential participation and elite status by drawing data from the general public and from elite groups, much greater effort in comparative studies needs to be devoted to the linkages between representatives and represented. Our investigation has documented in one context the profound composition of legislative support across the political hierarchy. In future studies, great profit would accrue to research which demonstrated the construction of legislative support in the nexus between the legislator and his constituents. Especially in less developed systems, the legislative body may not be sufficiently salient for those in the mass public to have acquired supportive orientations to it as an institution. There, the viability of the institution may depend very heavily upon the support constituents can give to their own representative. In Iowa, variations in the salience of the legislature did not differentiate the more supportive from the less supportive, but Iowa is a site in which the salience of the legislature is generally very high. The less politically developed context may present opportunities that were unavailable with Iowa samples to probe the relationships between representative-constituent linkages and the pattern of development of diffuse support for the legislature.

Certainly our general strategy for assessing the effects of independent variables upon diffuse support for the legislature can be replicated straightforwardly in other research settings. Our own explanatory model, appropriate for the explanation of variation in support in the Iowa context, will, however, undoubtedly be elaborated and perfected when comparative analyses are undertaken. We believe there is a reasonable theoretical payoff to be expected in undertaking comparative research of this kind.

NOTES

1. Other reports from the Iowa Legislative Research Project are: Boynton, Patterson and Hedlund (1968), Boynton and Patterson (1969), Patterson, Boynton and Hedlund (1969), Patterson and Boynton (1969), and Patterson, Wahlke and Boynton (1973).

2. The Iowa Legislative Research Project was supported by grants and other research assistance from the National Science Foundation, the Social Science Research Council, the Research Department of the Des Moines *Register and Tribune,* the University of Iowa Graduate College and Computer Center, and the Laboratory for Political Research, Department of Political Science, University of Iowa. The principal investigators for this project were Samuel C. Patterson, G. Robert Boynton, and Ronald D. Hedlund.

3. For a different treatment of these data, see Patterson, Boynton and Hedlund (1969: 62-76).

4. Because two of the items in Table 8 did not produce unambiguous factor loadings ("friendly toward others" and "just an average citizen") they were omitted from further analysis.

5. Part of this analysis has been presented previously, in Patterson and Boynton (1969: 243-263).

6. Four variables are included in the regression analysis which have not been discussed in this chapter. They have been omitted from discussion because the results of their analysis did not turn out to be particularly interesting intrinsically; they bore only very trivial zero-order correlations with legislative support, and they contributed almost nothing to the overall multiple regression analysis. The four variables referred to respondents' general impressions of the job the legislature does—whether they thought of it largely as a law-making machine, whether they conceived of it mainly in terms of representation, whether they were able to see it as a place where specific kinds of policies are made, or whether they thought of it largely as a place where people are "in motion"—working hard, taking care of problems, and the like. We have presented some of this evidence in Boynton, Patterson and Hedlund (1969: 700-721).

REFERENCES

BLOM, R. (1970) "Public opinion about the functioning of social institutions." Acta Sociologica (2): 110-126.

BOYNTON, G.R., S.C. PATTERSON, and R.D. HEDLUND. (1968) "The structure of public support for legislative institutions." Midwest Journal of Political Science (May): 163-173.

BOYNTON, G.R. and S.C. PATTERSON. (1969) "The missing links in legislative politics: attentive constituents." J. of Politics (August): 700-721.

EASTON, D. (1965) A Systems Analysis of Political Life. New York: Wiley.

LOWENBERG, G. (1973) "The institutionalization of parliament and public orientations to the political system," in A. Kornberg (ed.) Legislatures in Comparative Perspective. New York: McKay.

——— (1971) "The influence of parliamentary behavior on regime stability: some conceptual clarifications." Comparative Politics (April): 177-200.

MULLER, E.N. (1970) "The representation of citizens by political authorities: consequences for regime support." American Political Science Rev. (December): 1149-1166.

NIX, H.L., D. McINTYRE and C.J. DUDLEY (1968) "Bases of leadership: the cultural ideal and estimates of reality." Southwestern Social Science Quarterly (December): 423-432.

PATTERSON, S.C. and G.R. BOYNTON (1969) "Legislative recruitment in a civic culture." Social Science Quarterly (September): 243-263.

PATTERSON, S.C., G.R. BOYNTON and R.D. HEDLUND (1969) "Perceptions and expectations of the legislature and support for it." American J. of Sociology (July): 62-76.

PATTERSON, S.C., J.C. WAHLKE and G.R. BOYNTON (1973) "Dimensions of support in legislative systems," in A. Kornberg (ed.) Legislatures in Comparative Perspective. New York: McKay.